Big Ray's

EVEN MORE ! BAD ASS

OLD TRUCKS! 2

Adult Coloring Book

THIS BOOK BELONGS TO

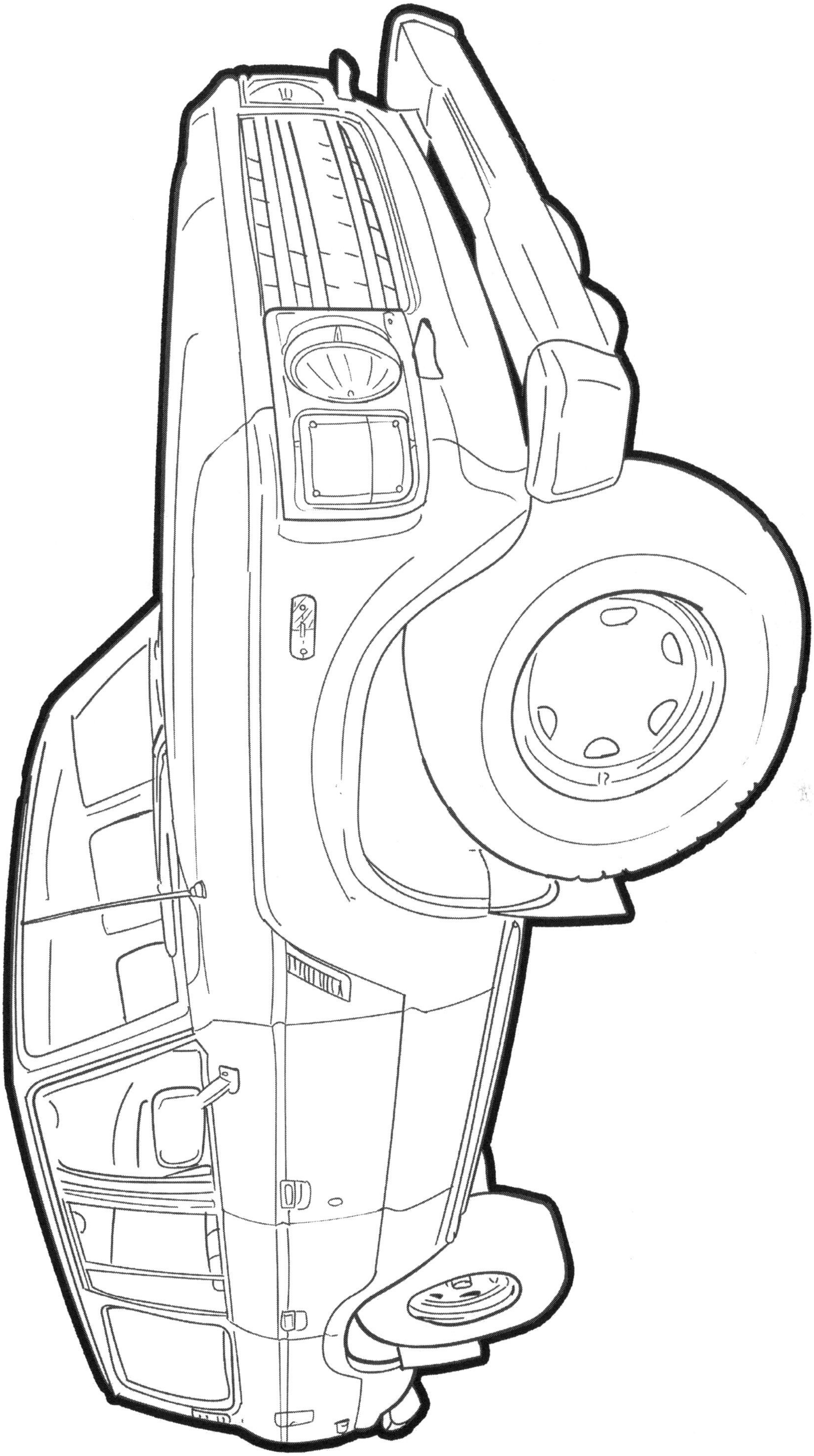

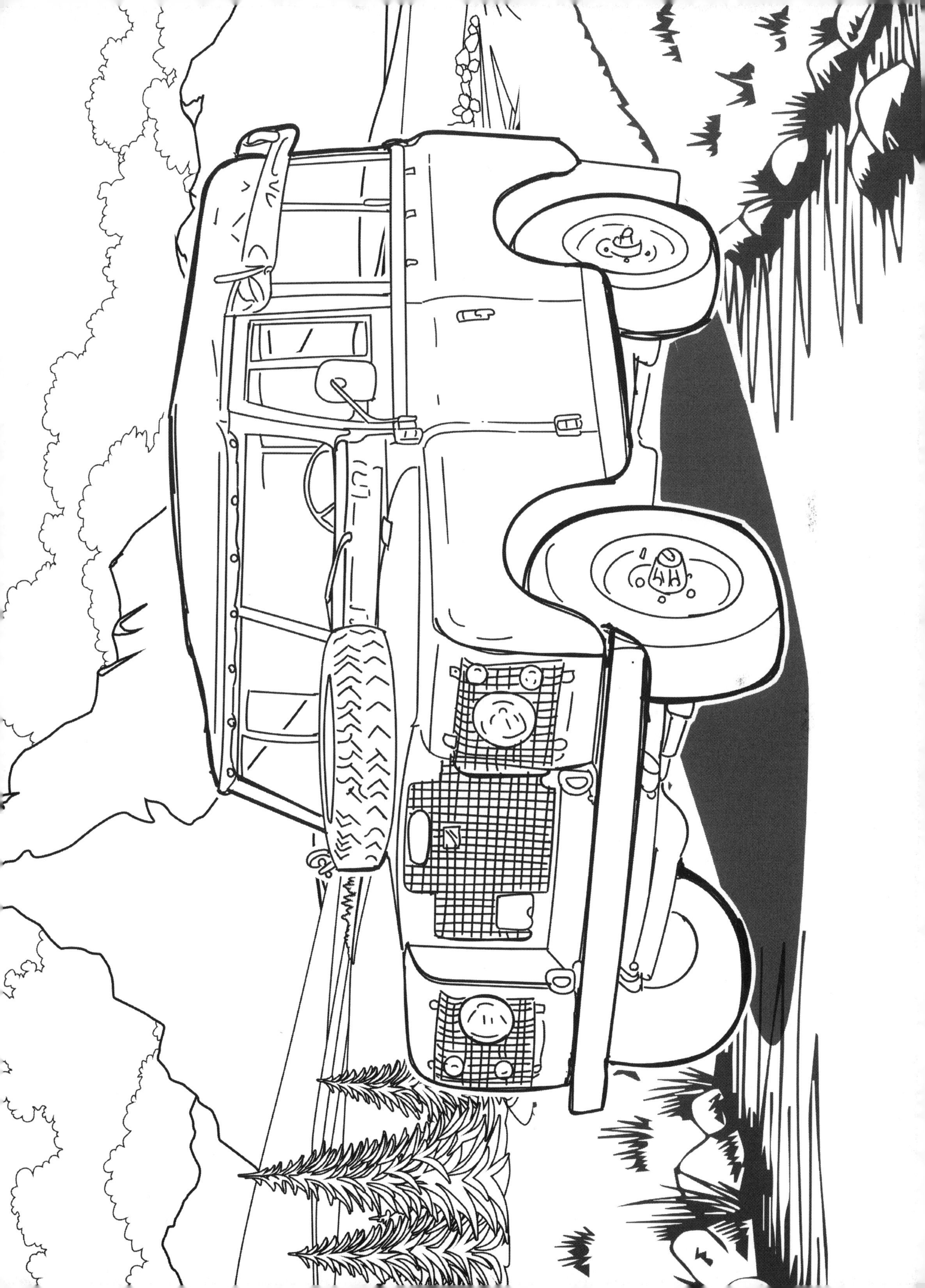

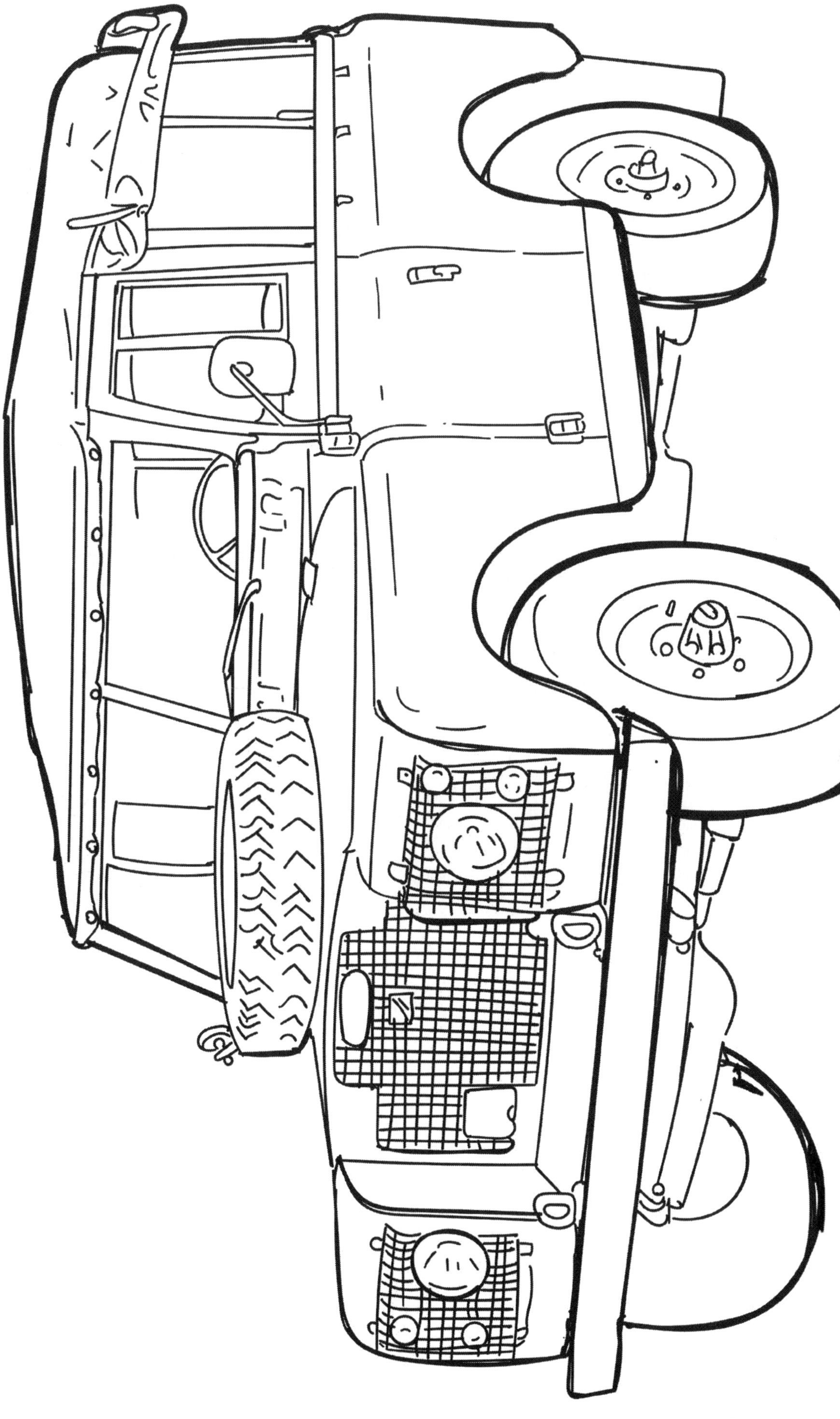

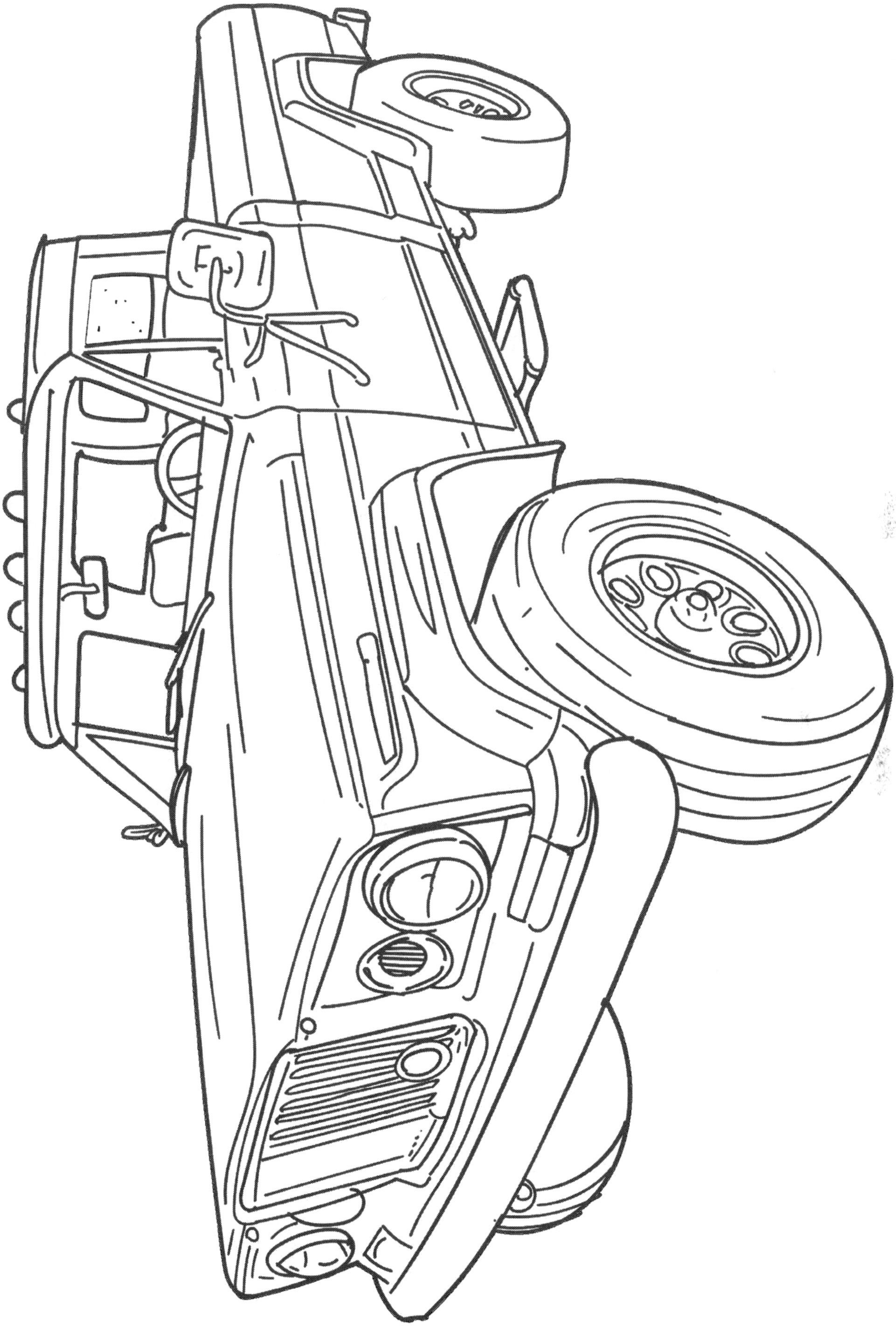

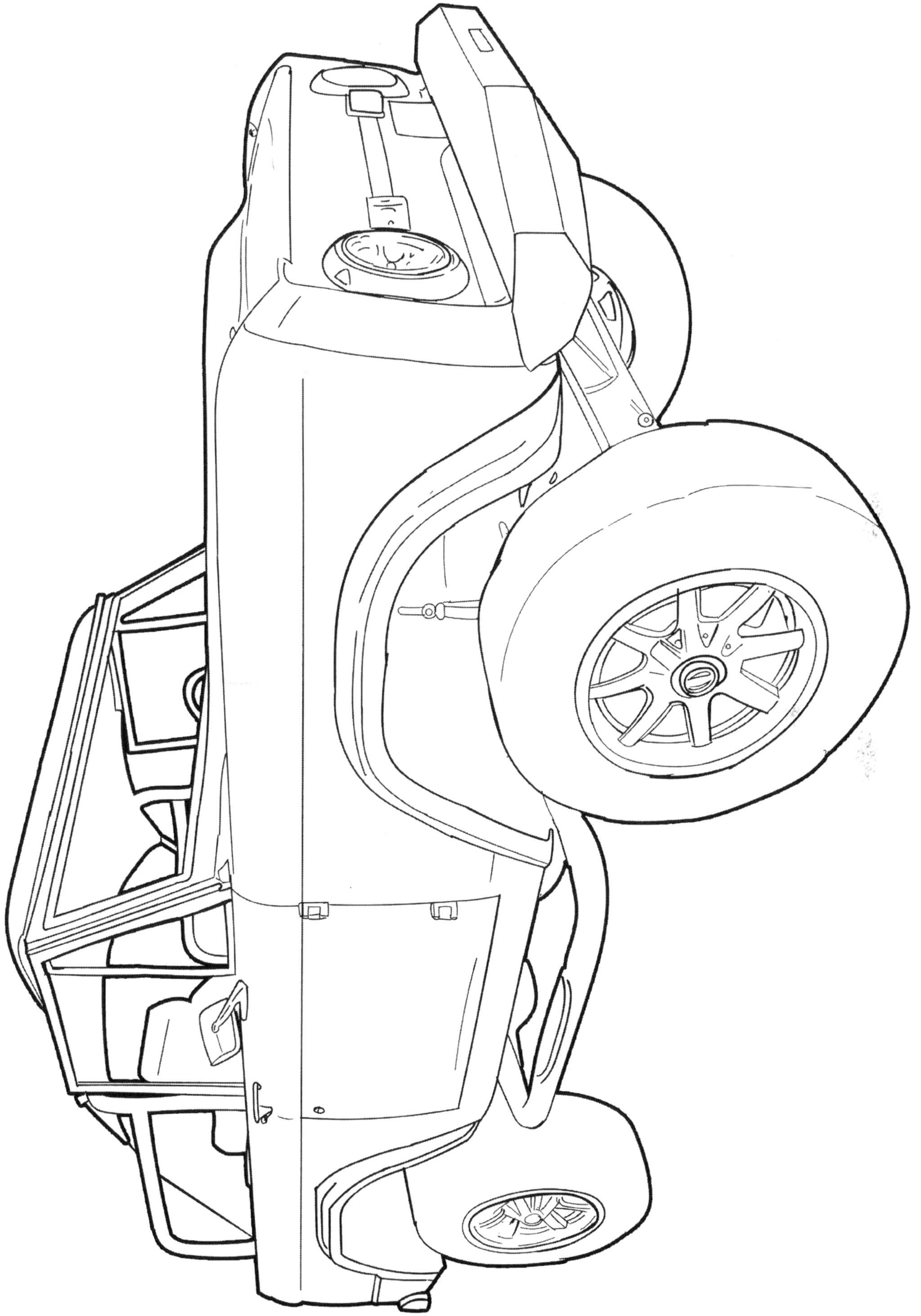

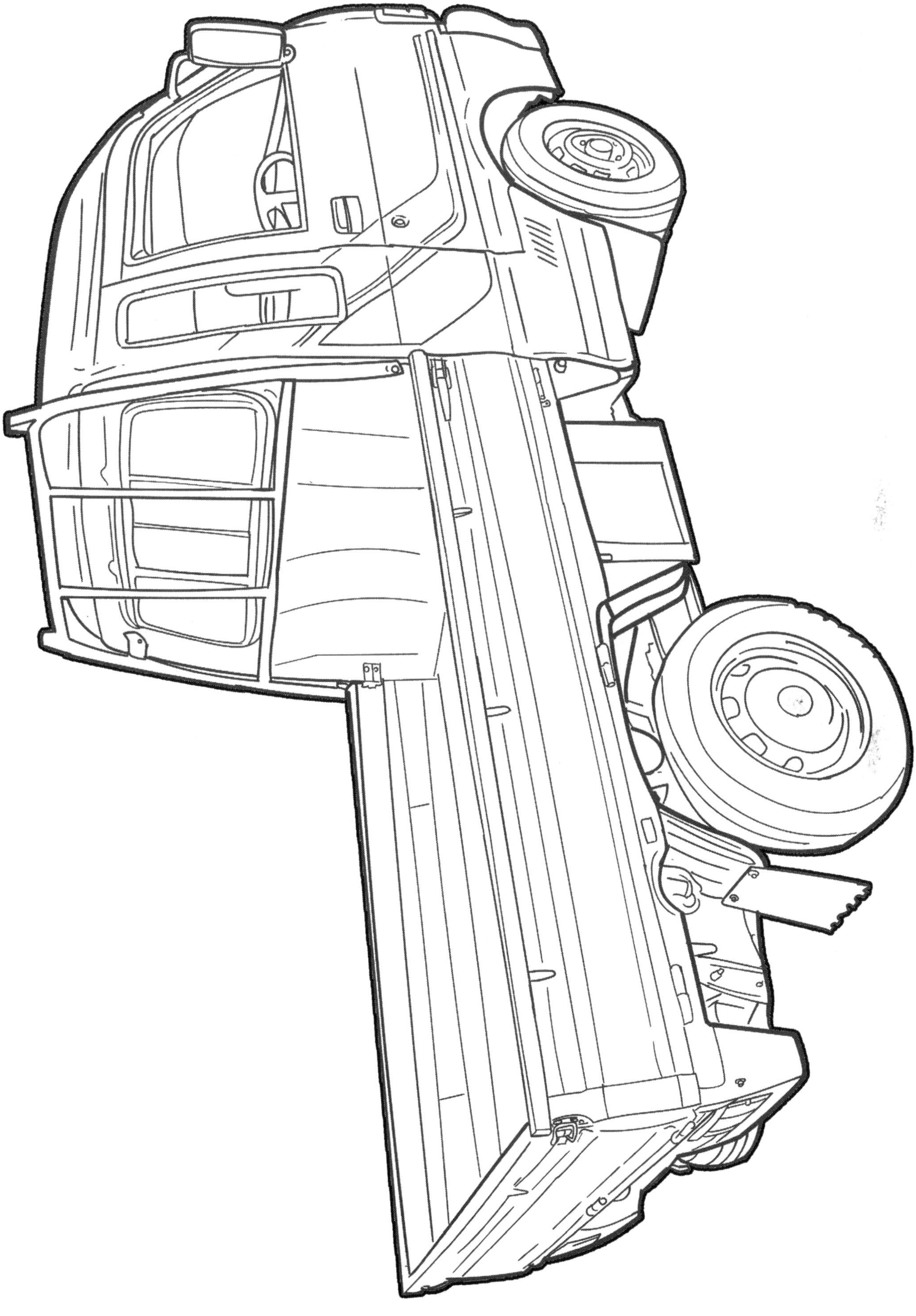

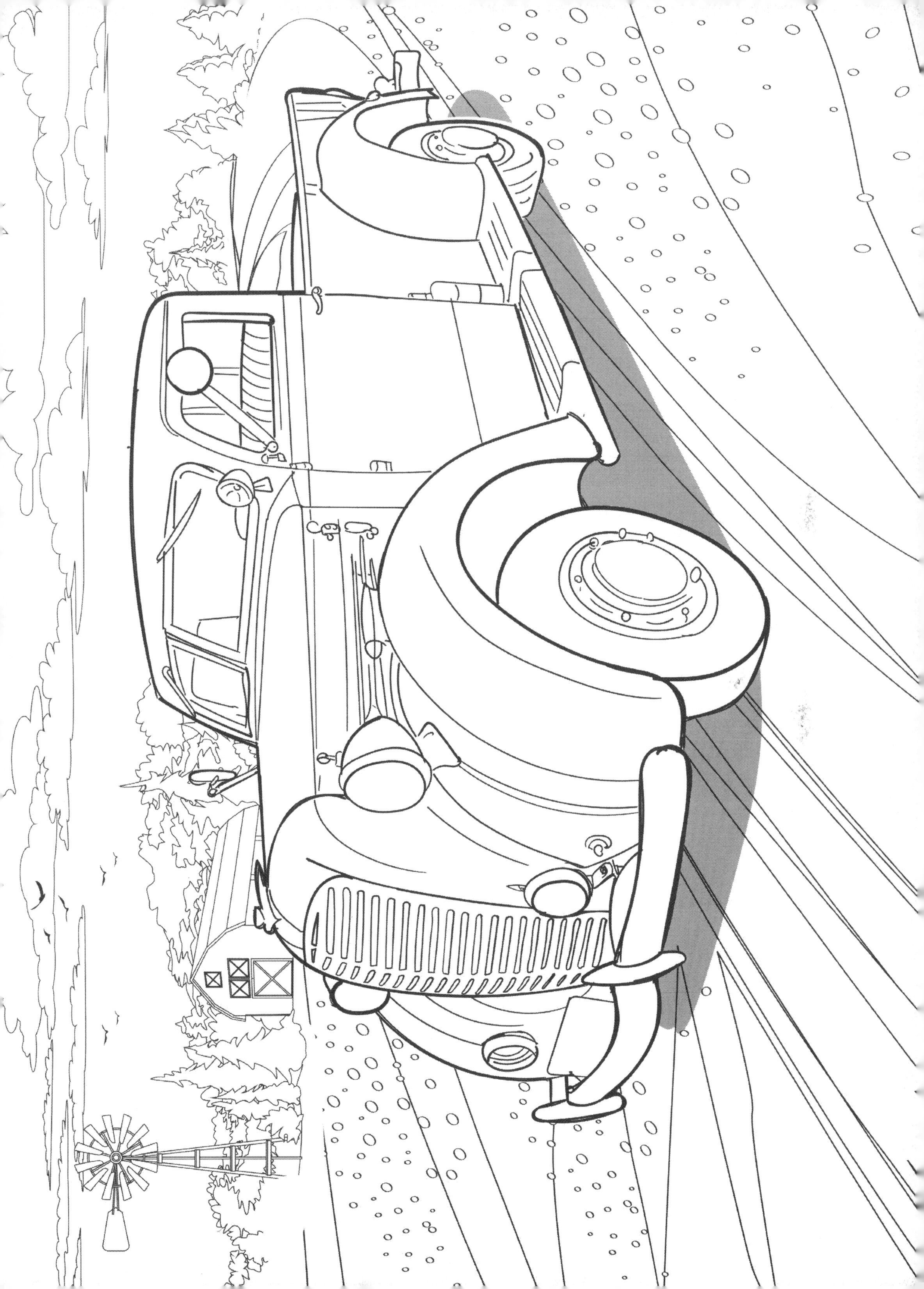

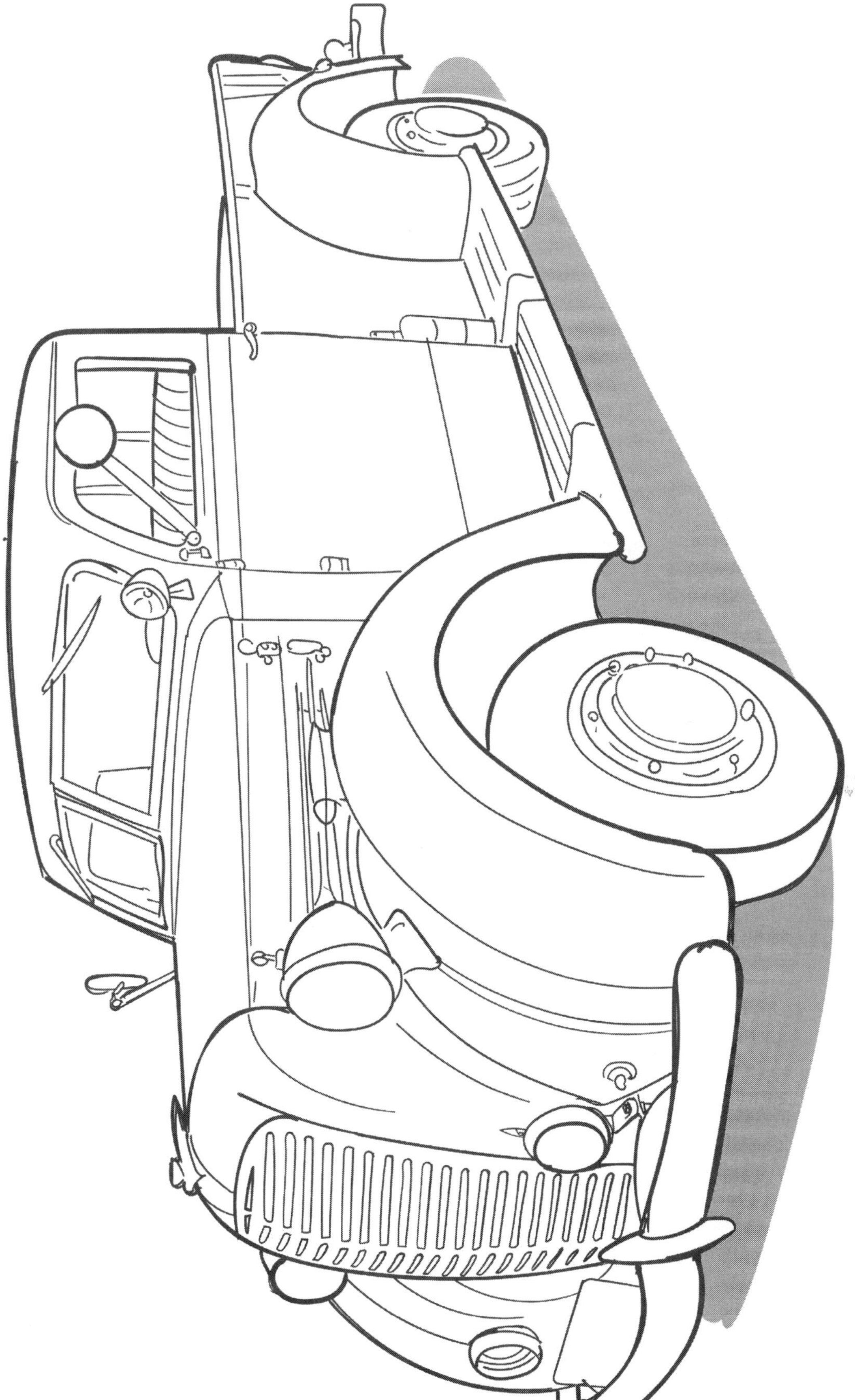

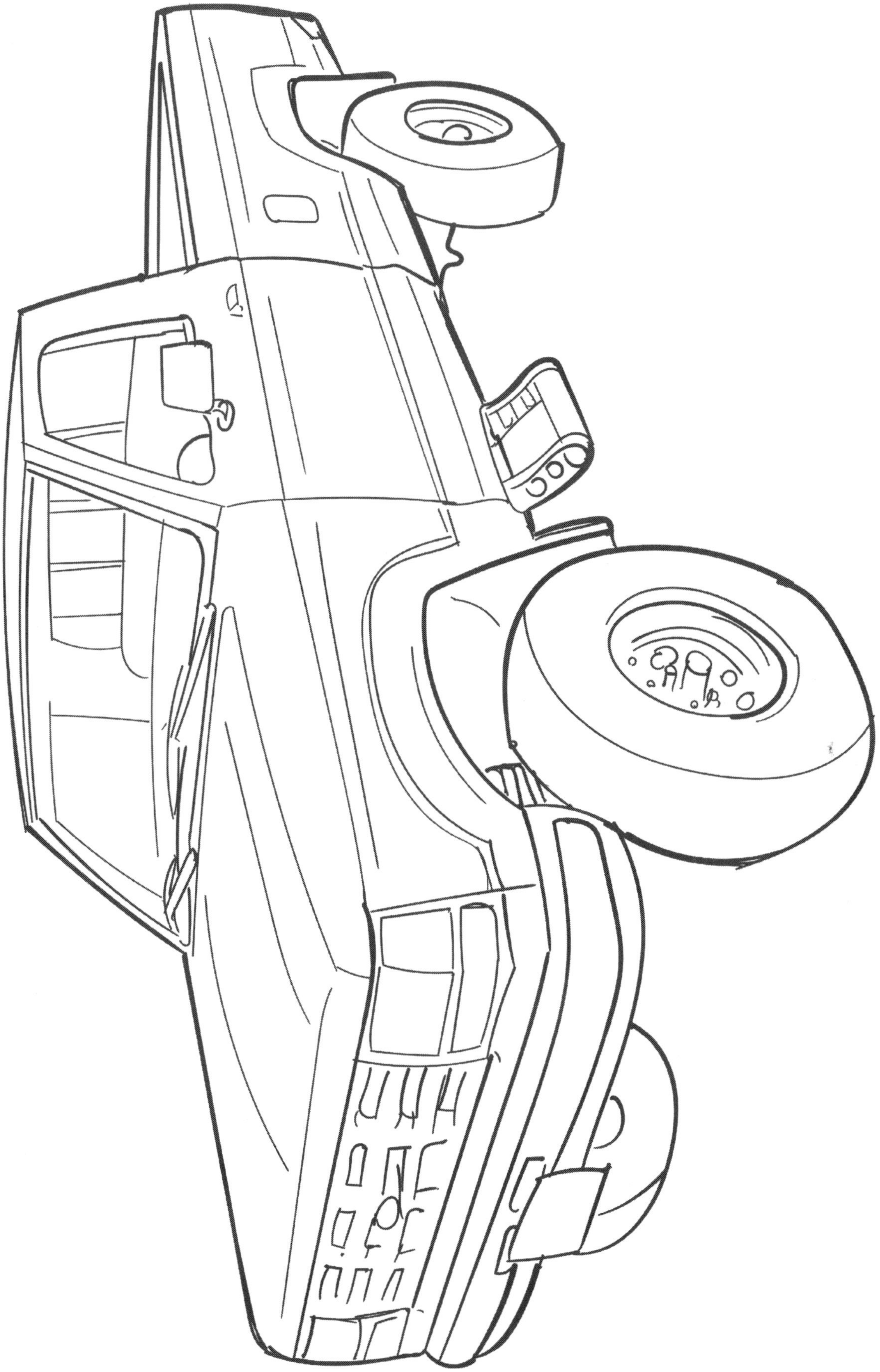

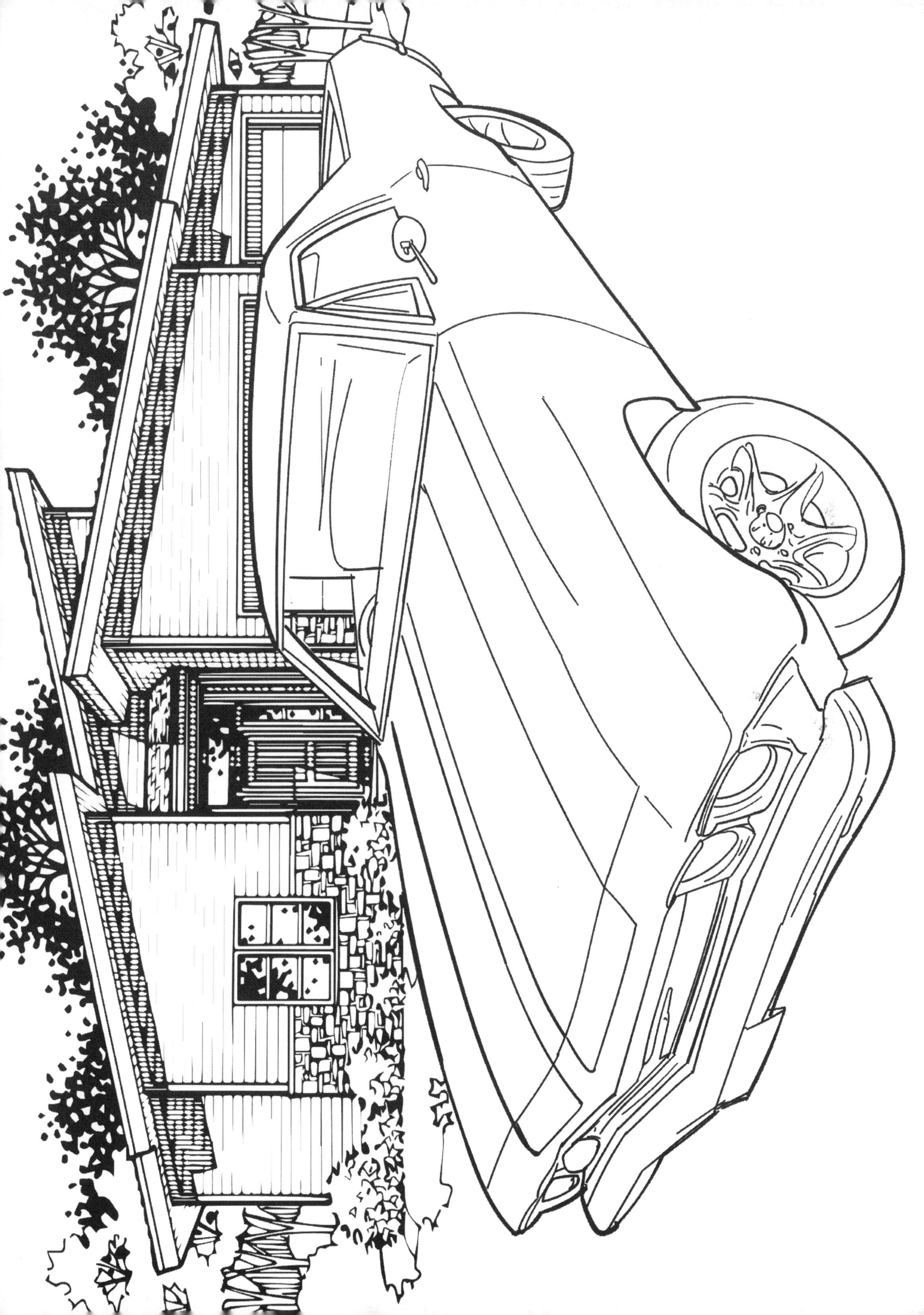

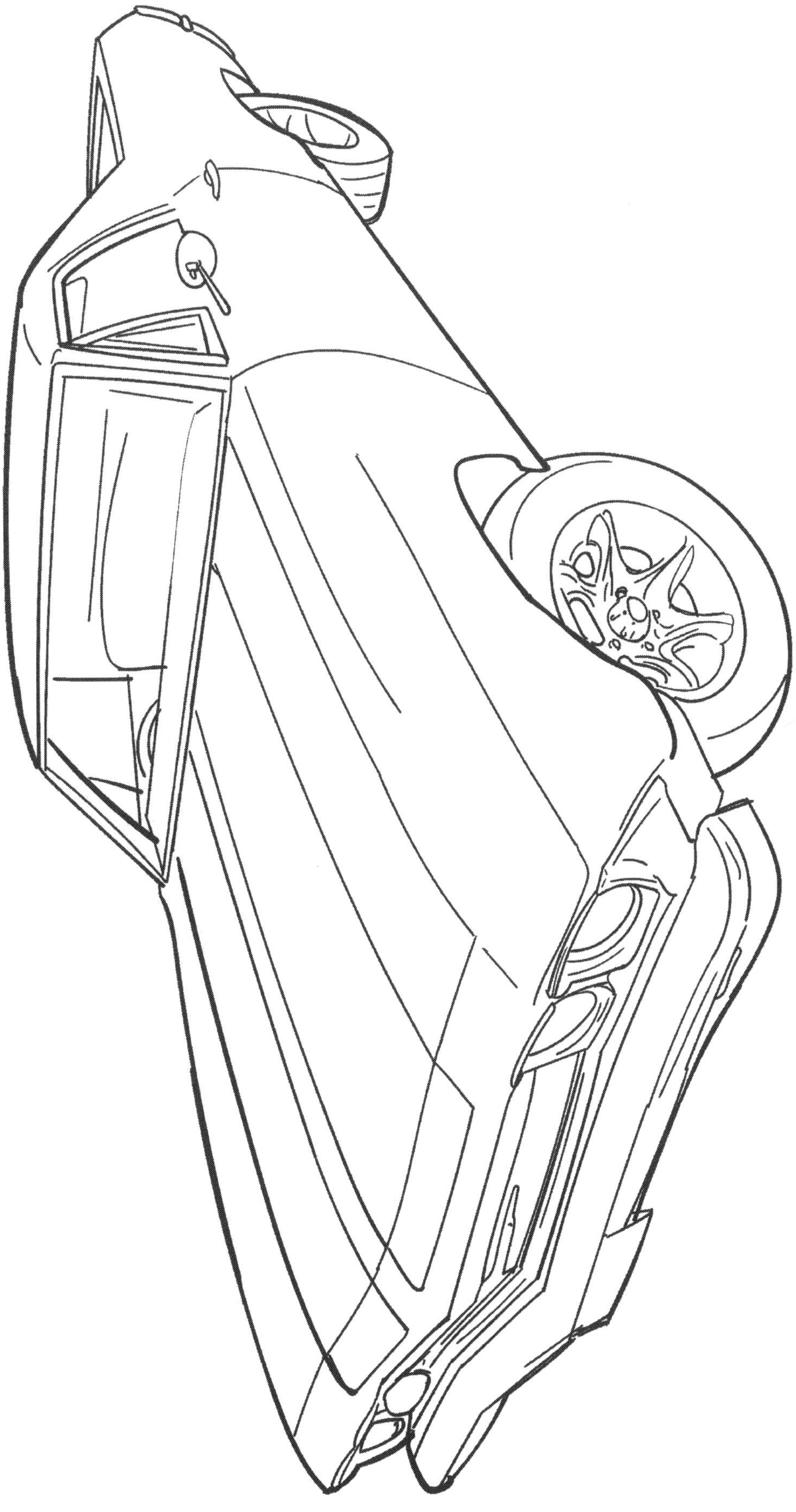

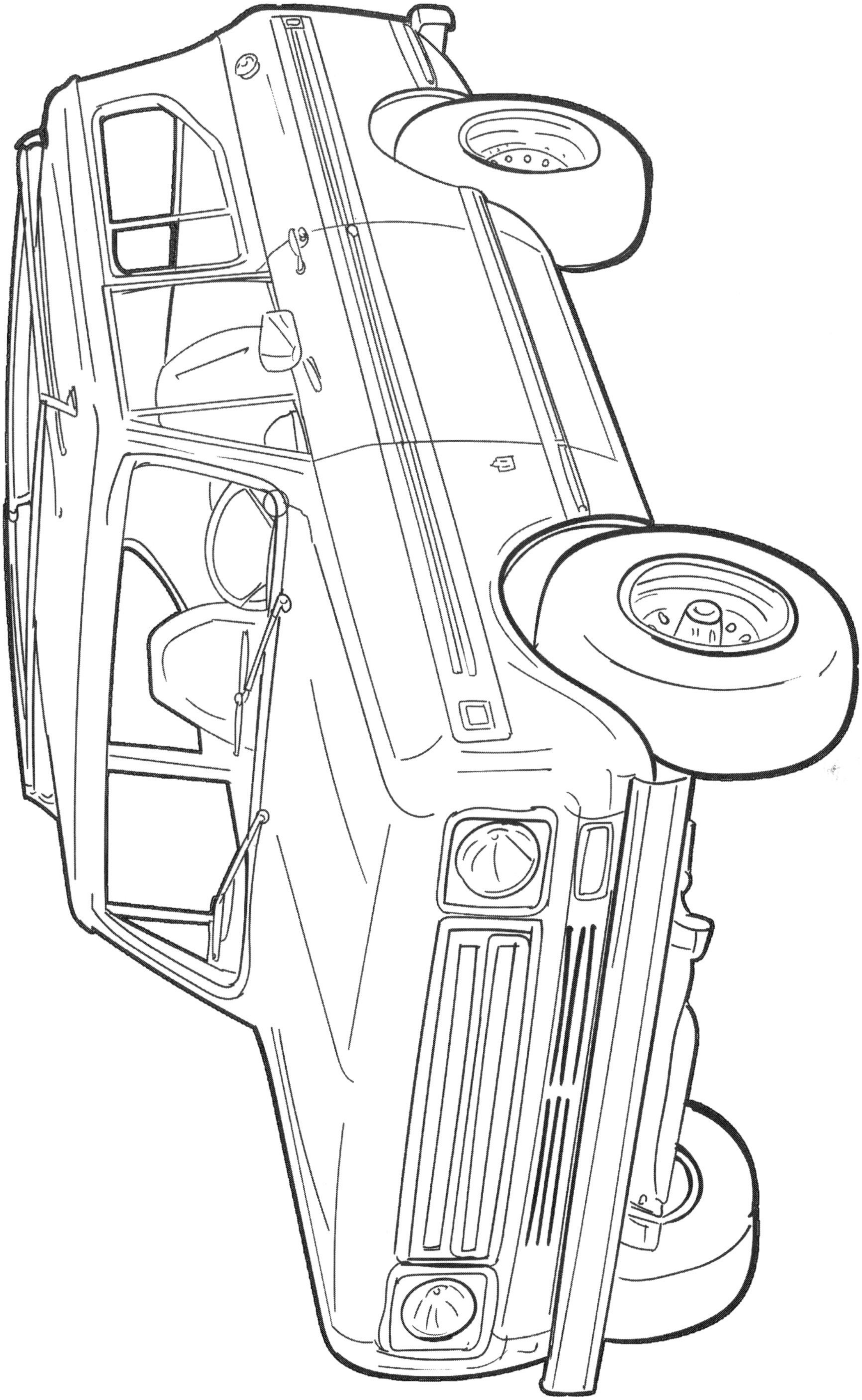

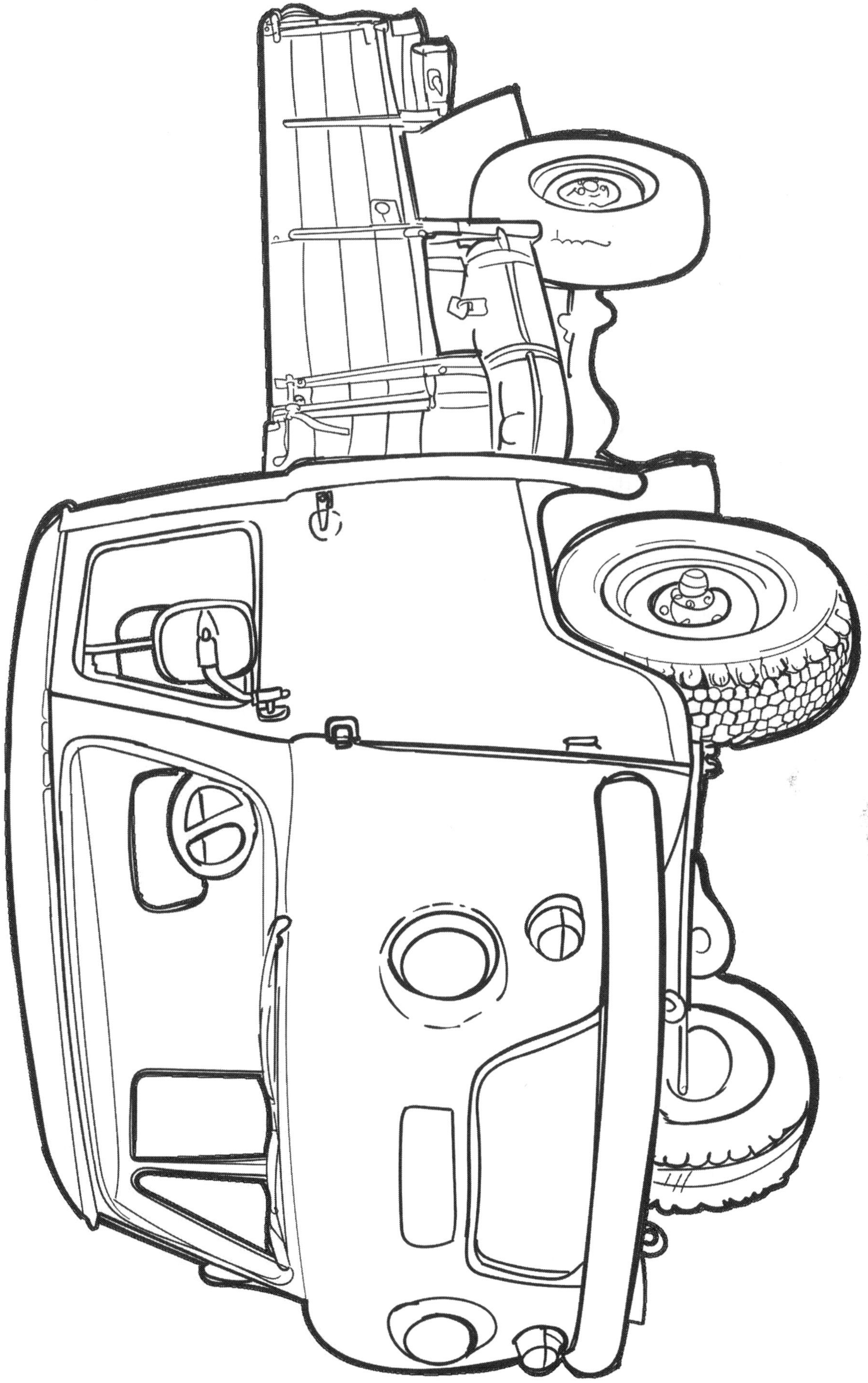

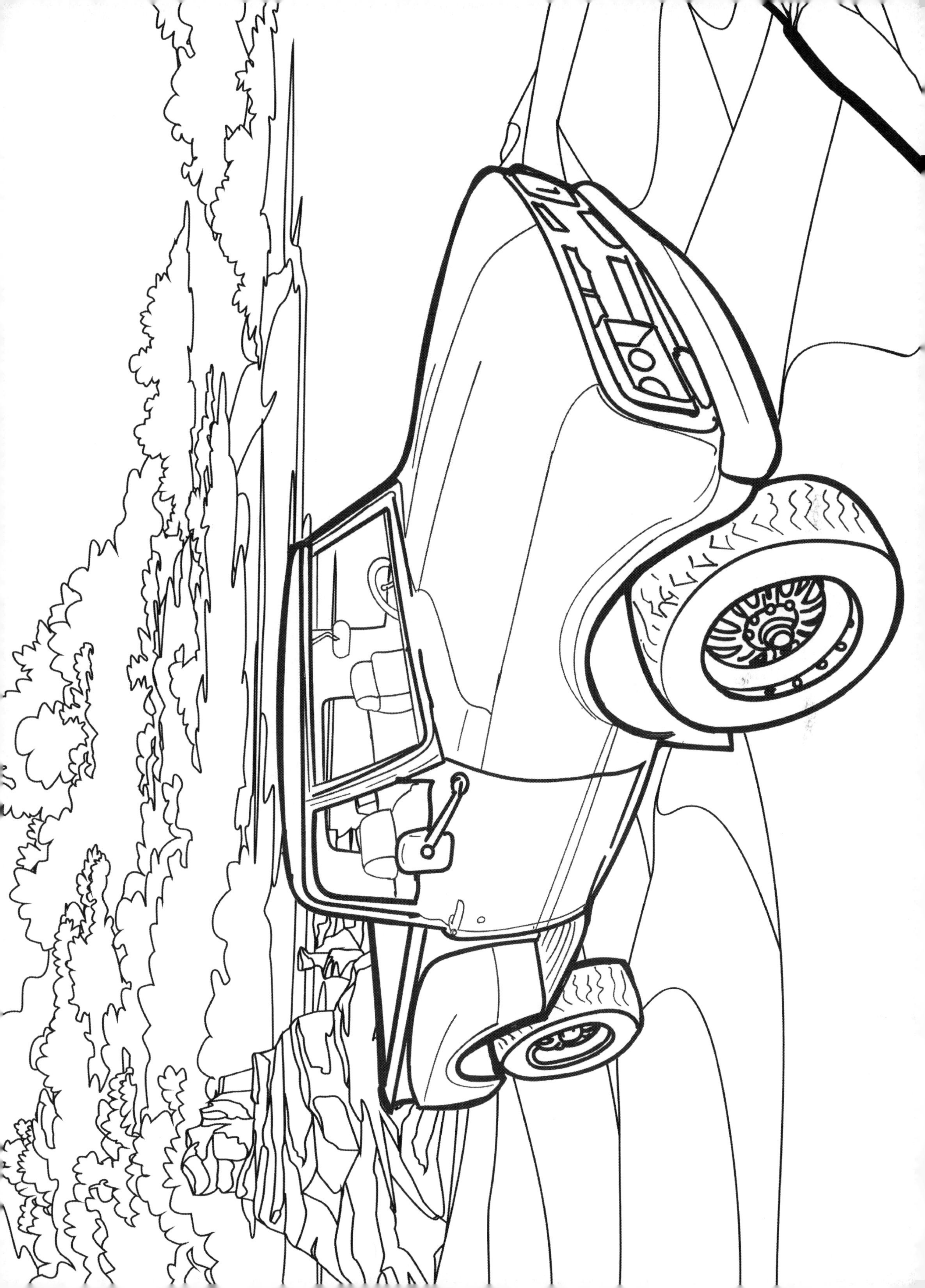

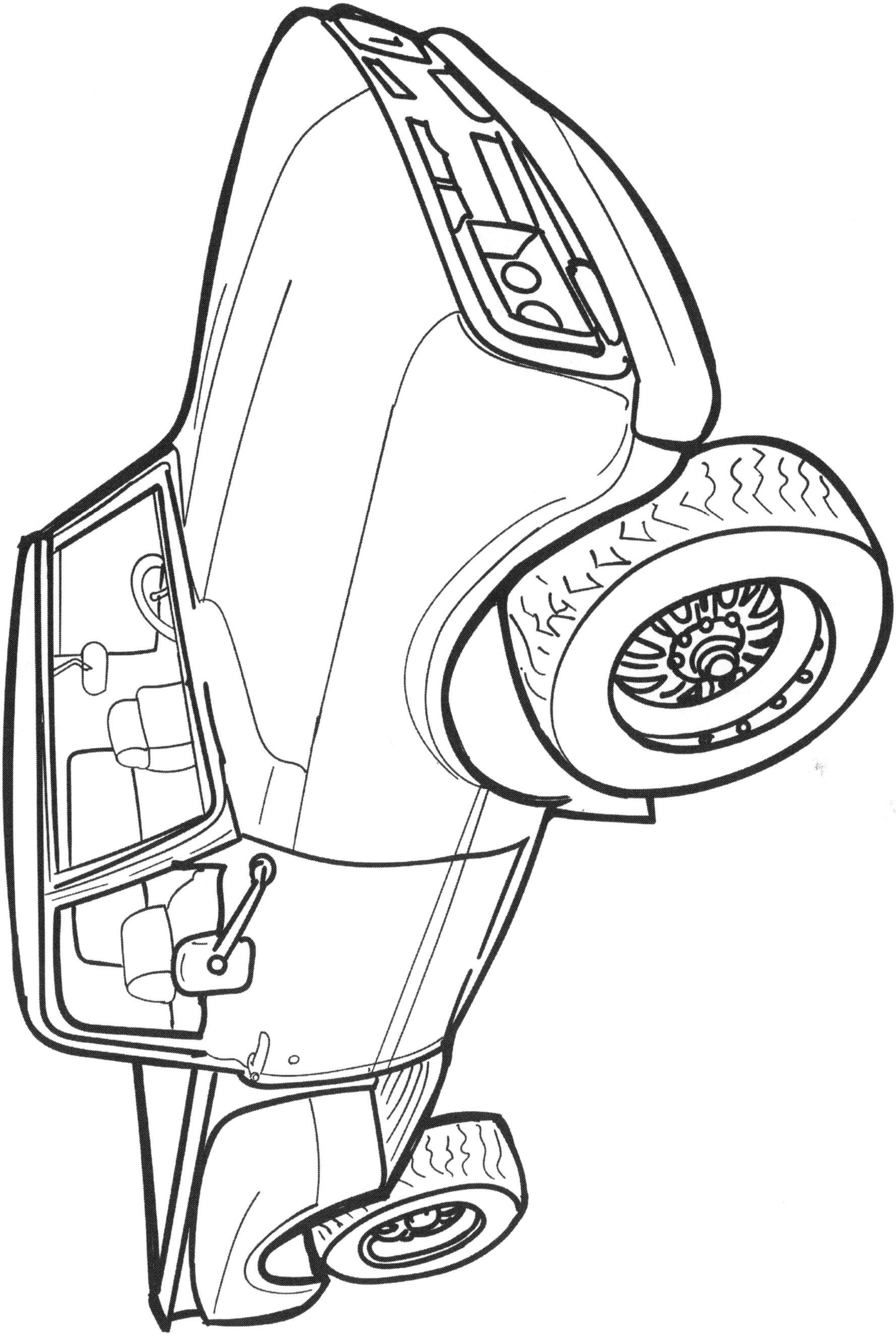

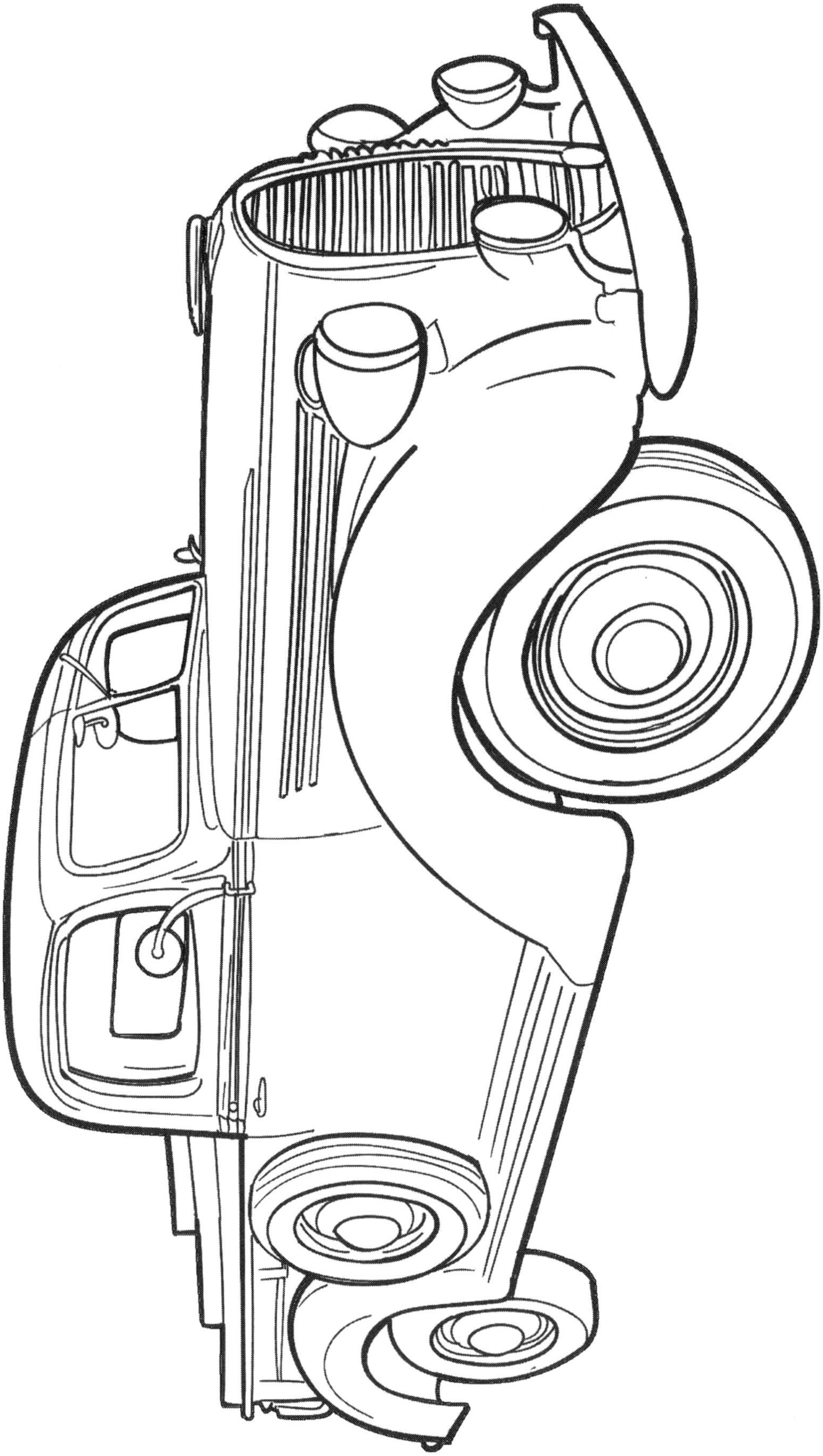

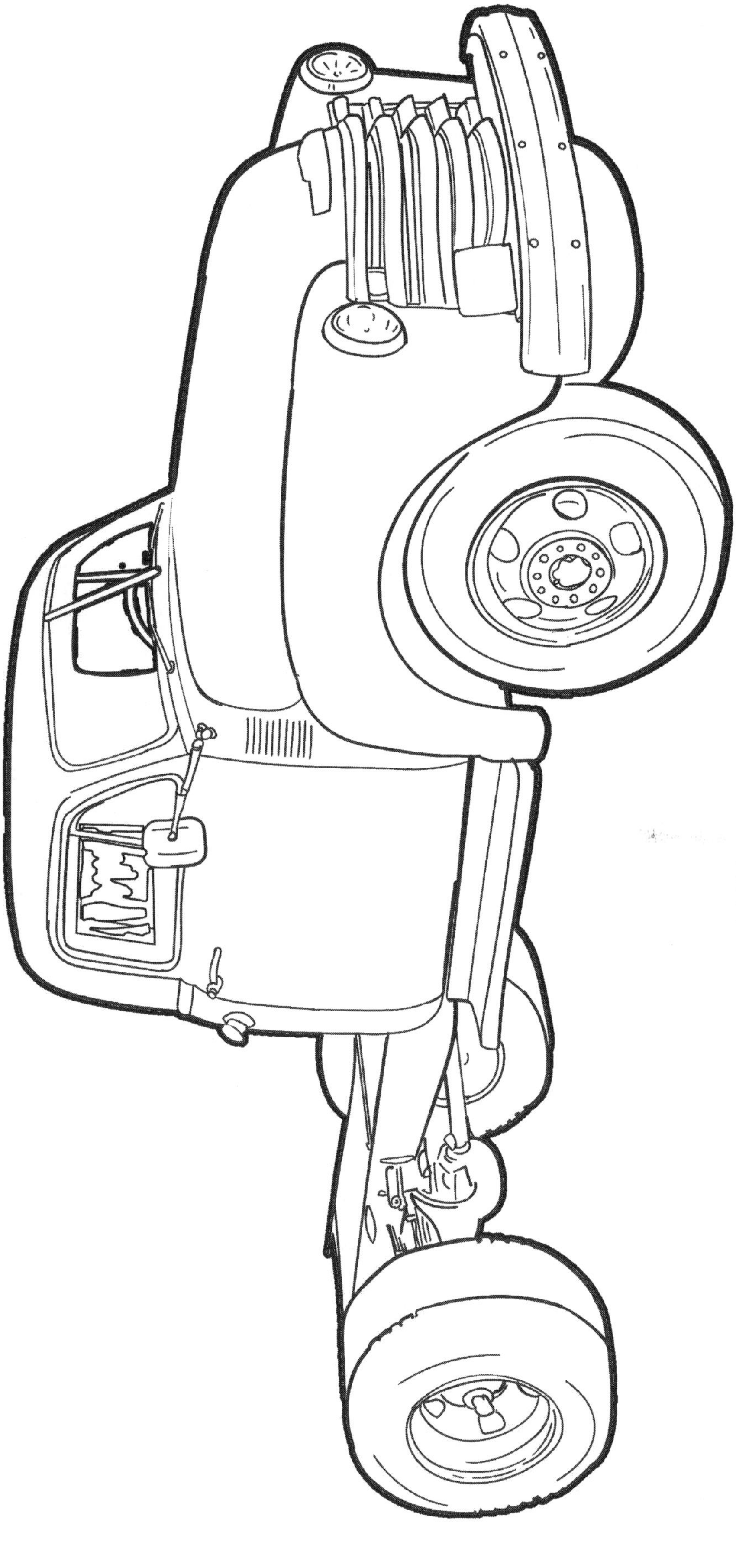

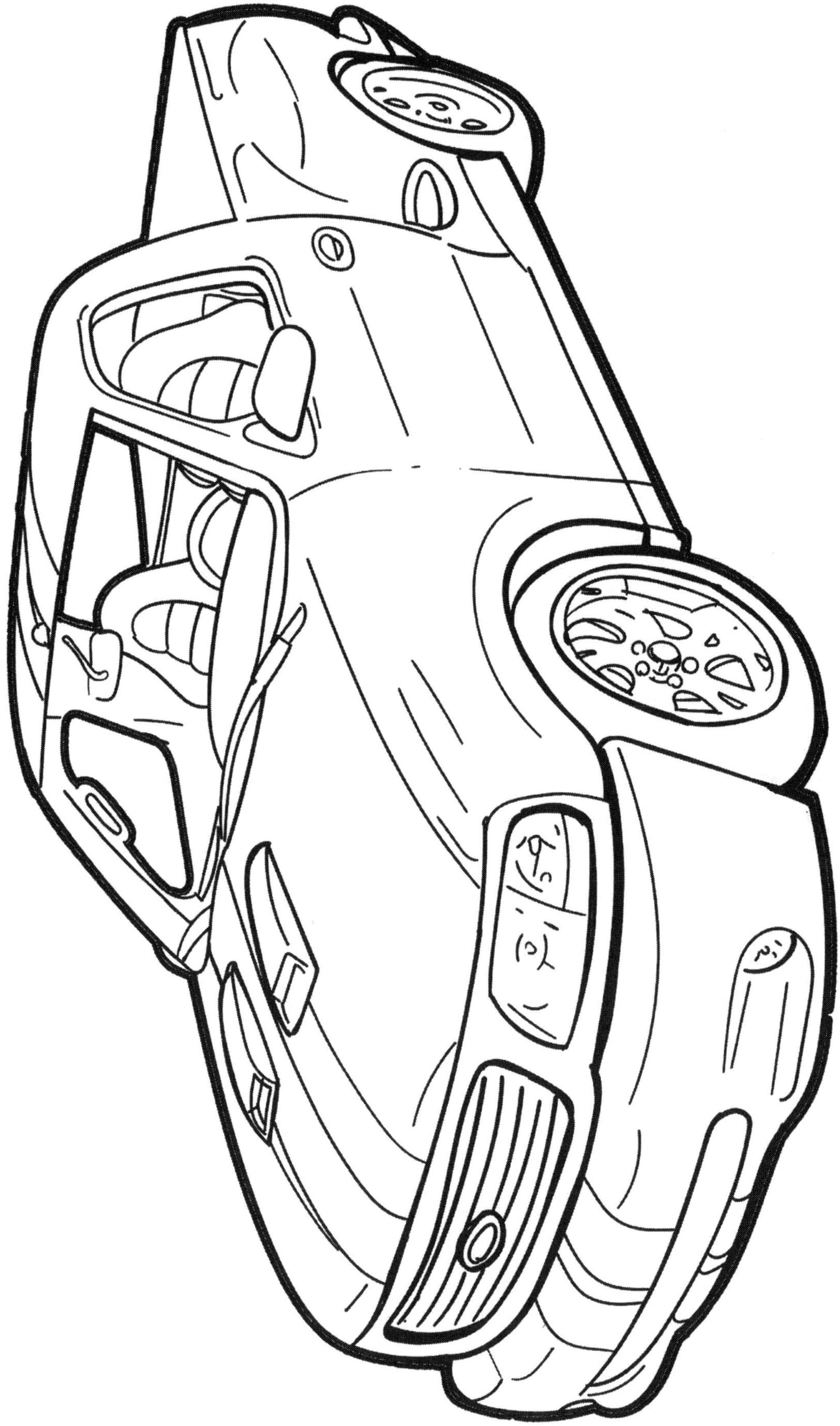

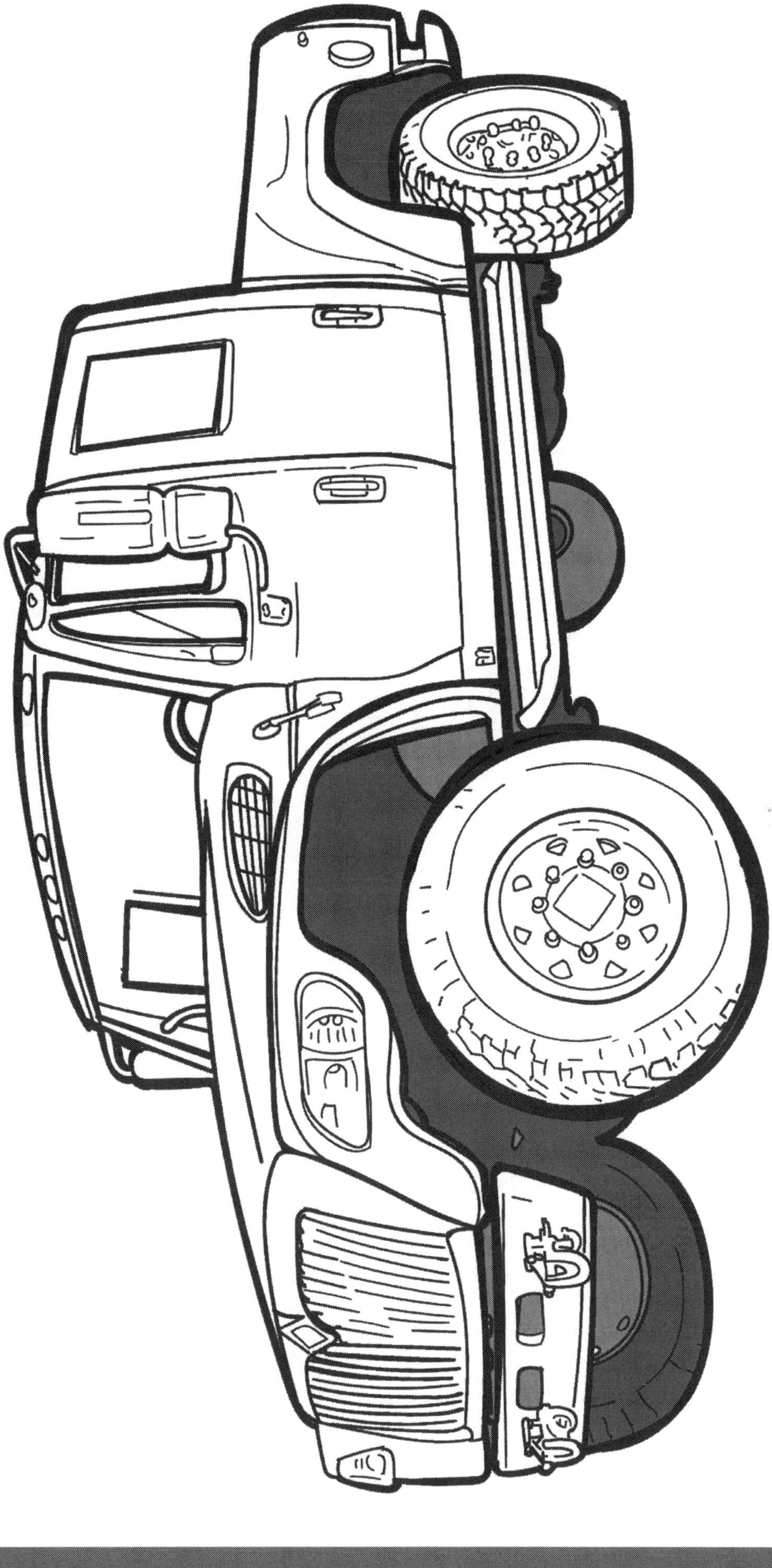

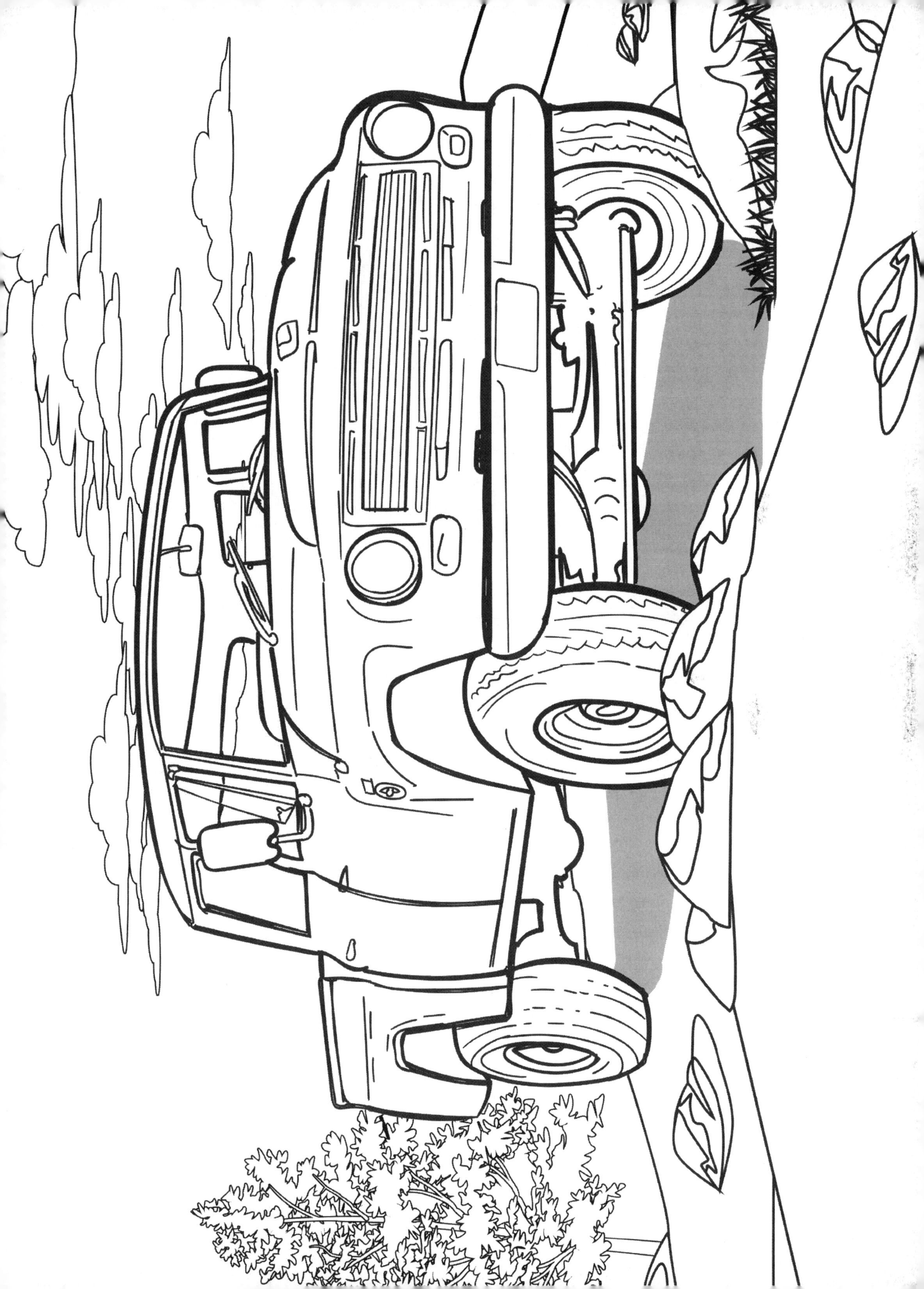

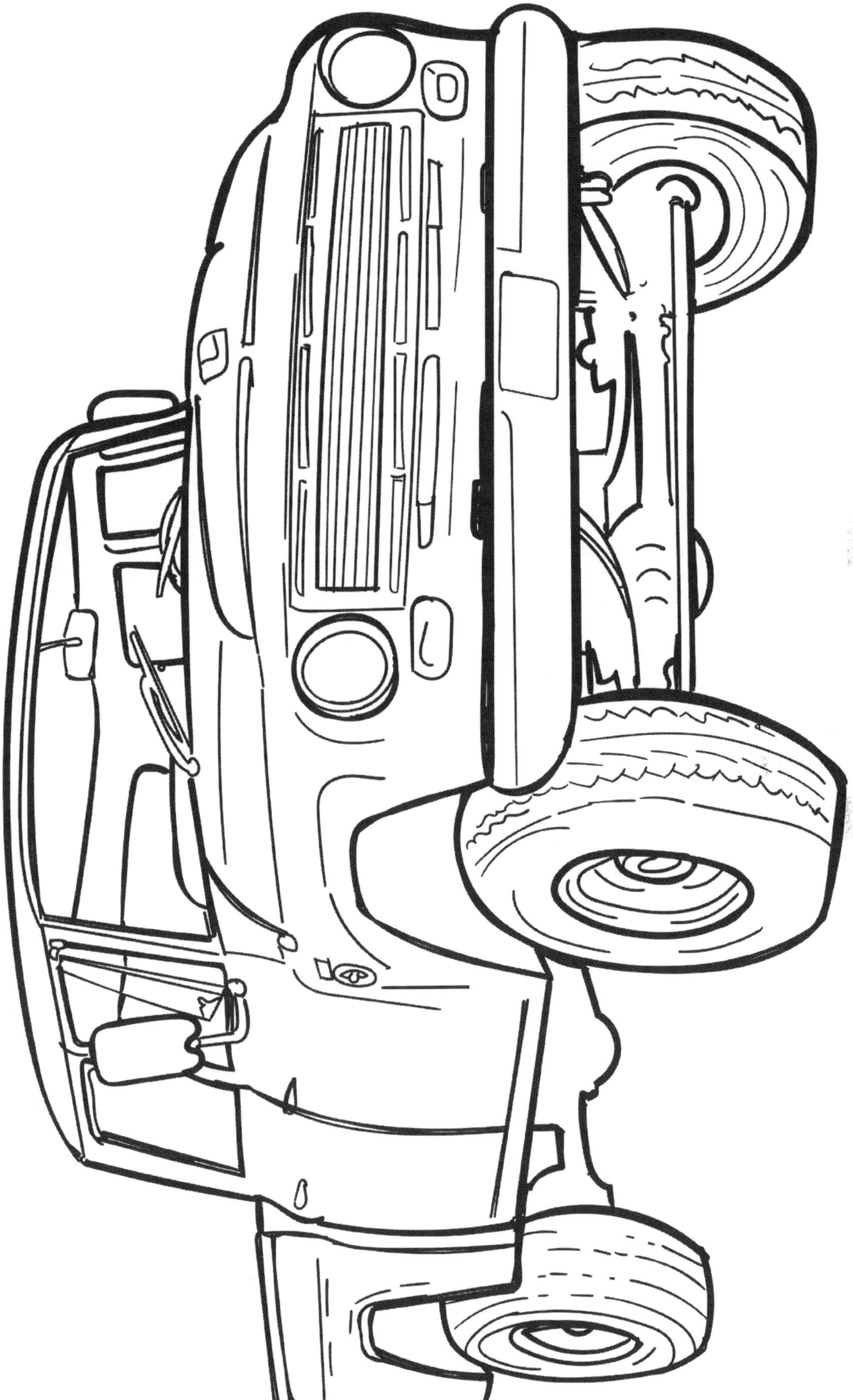

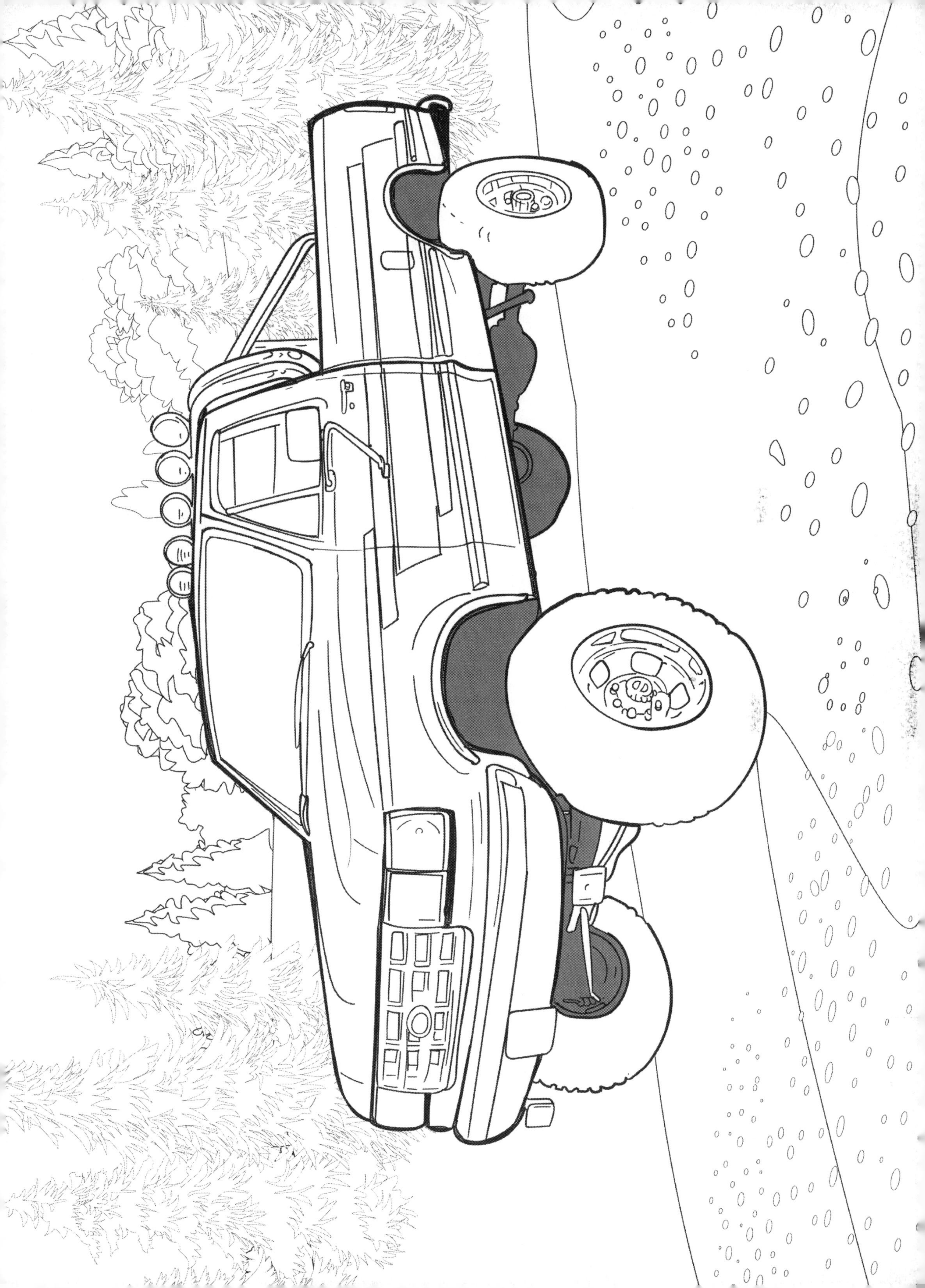

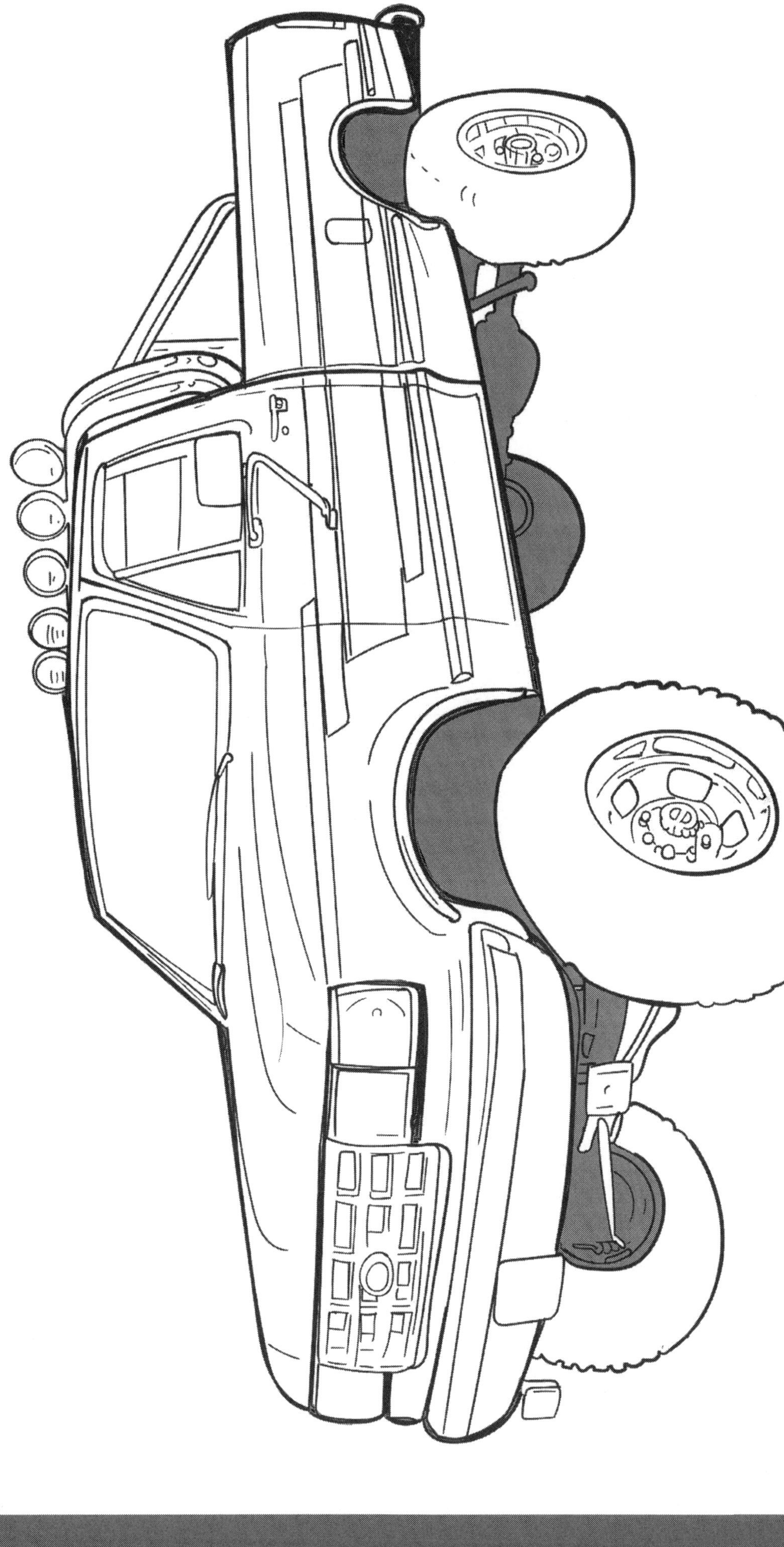

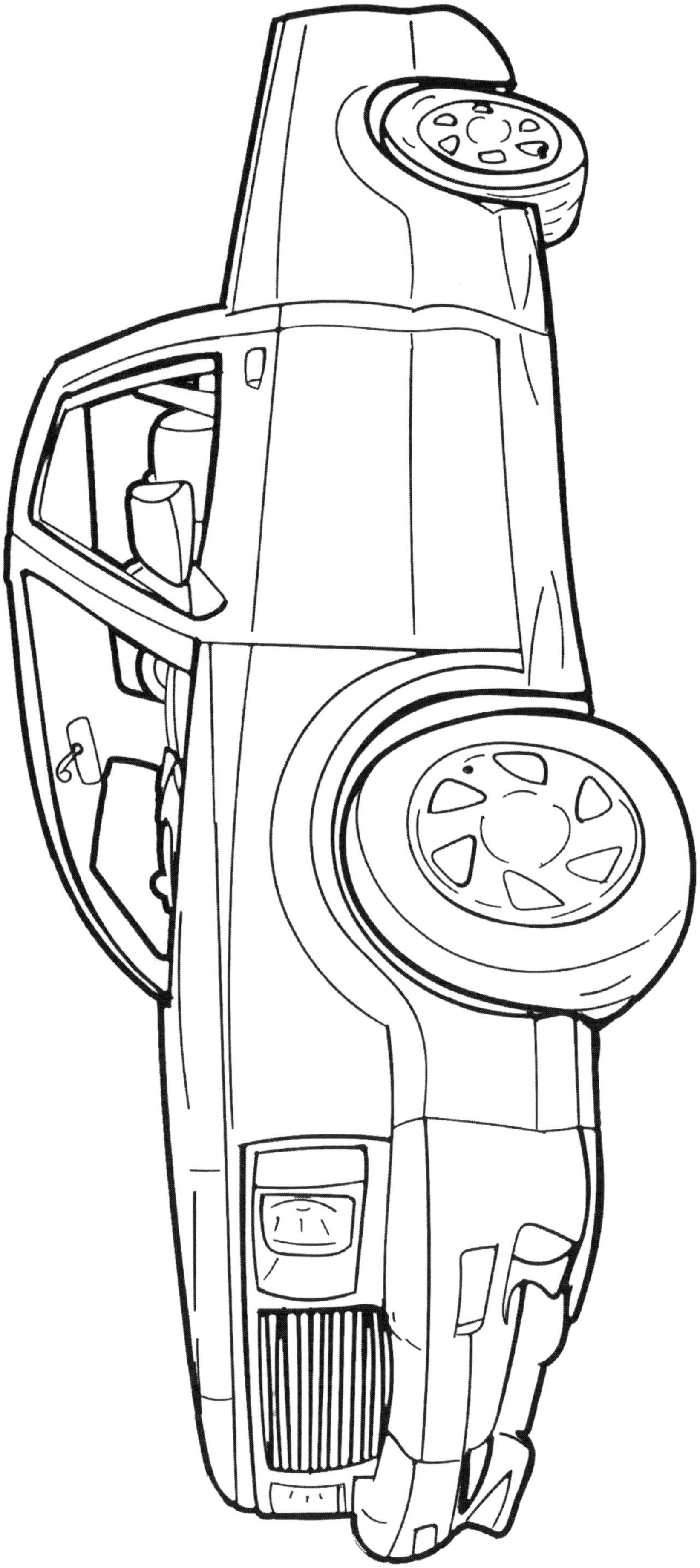

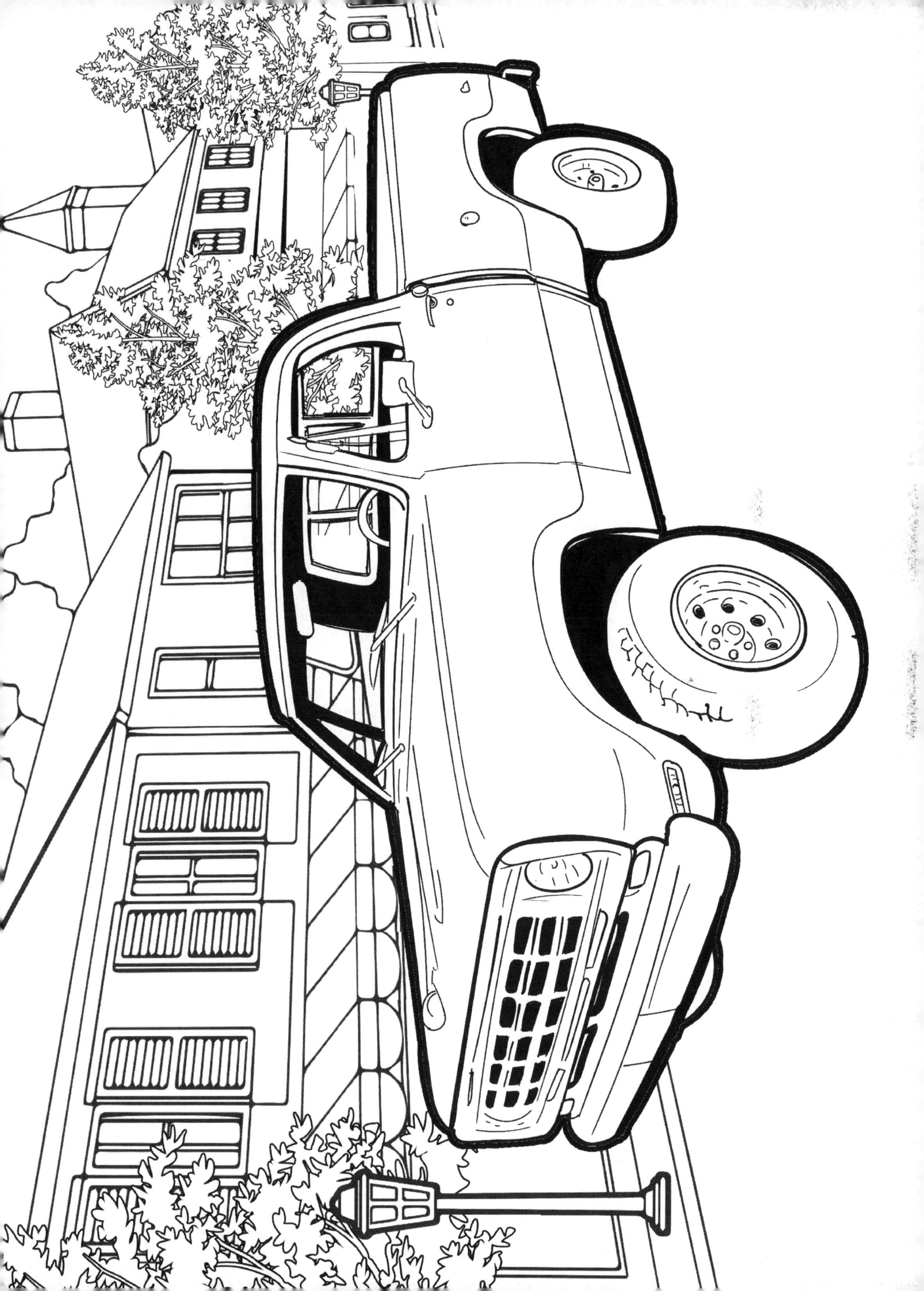

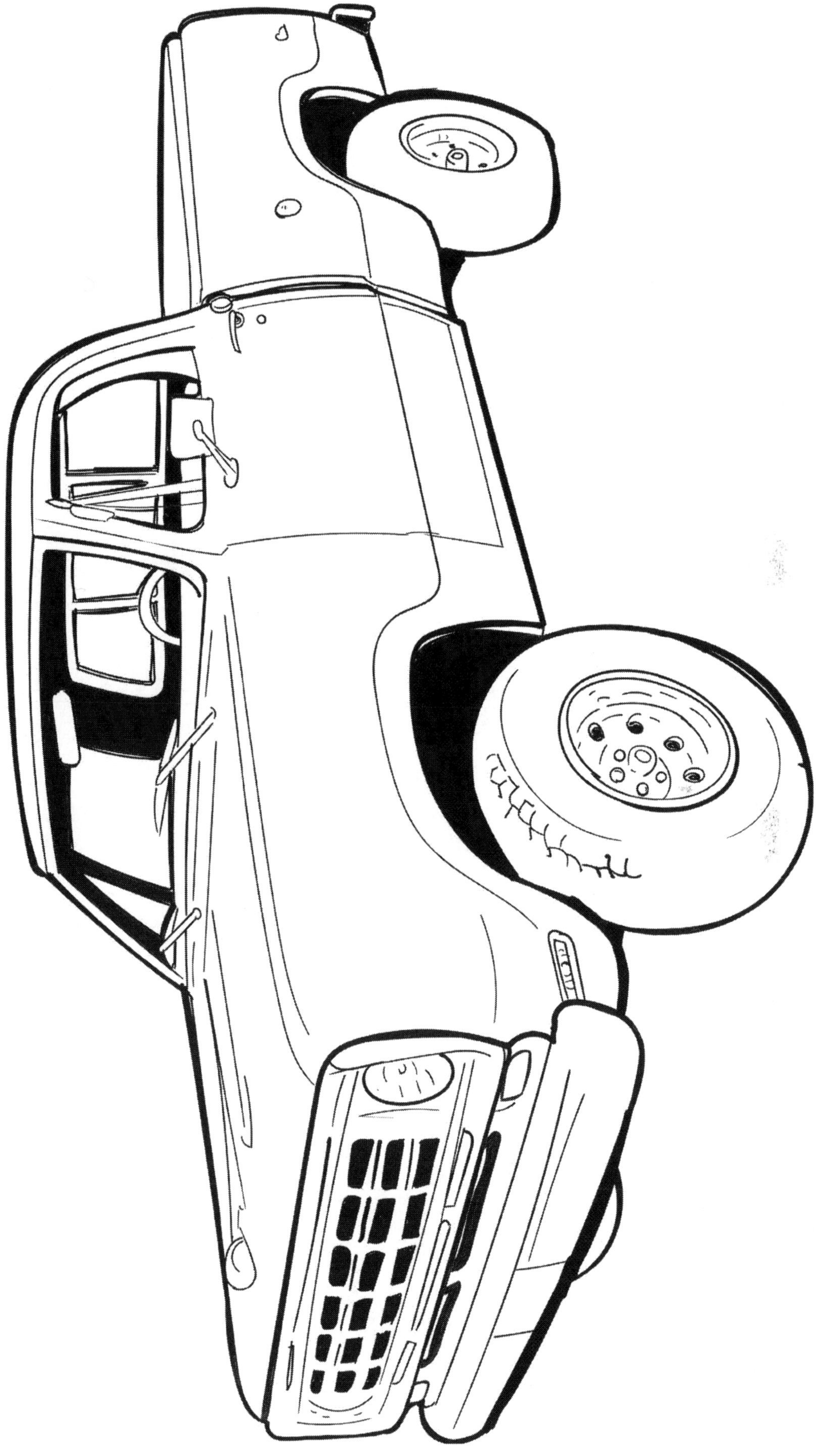

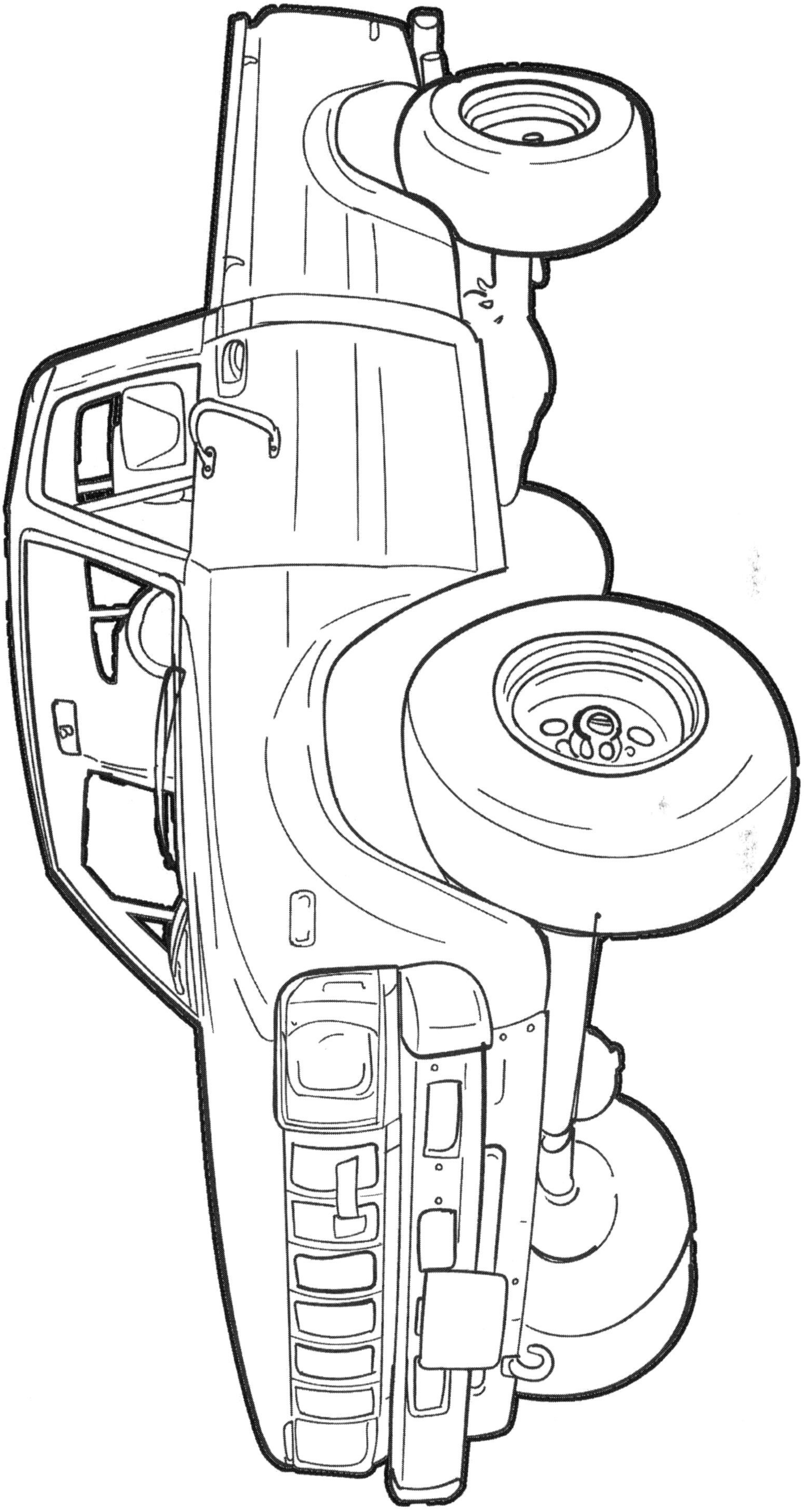

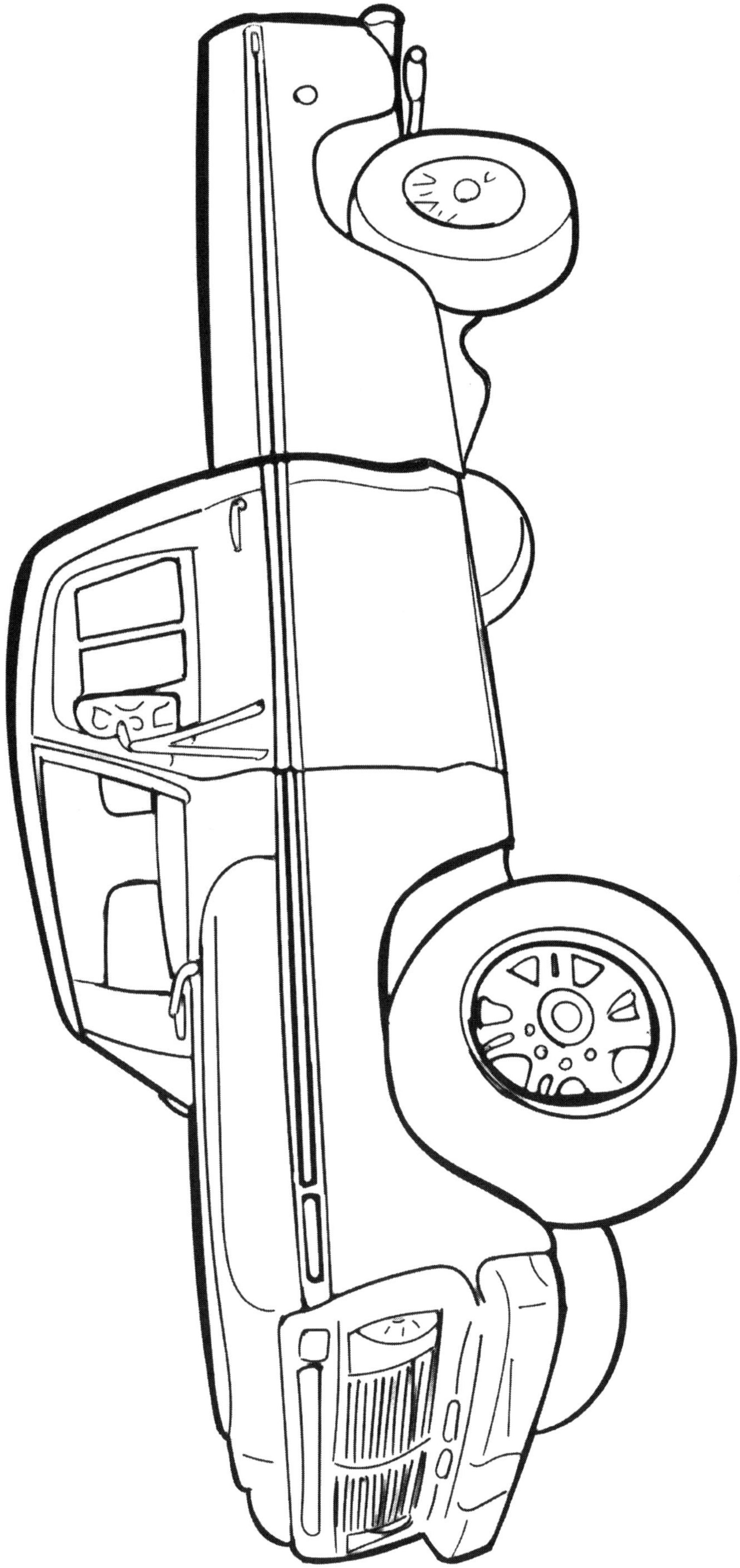

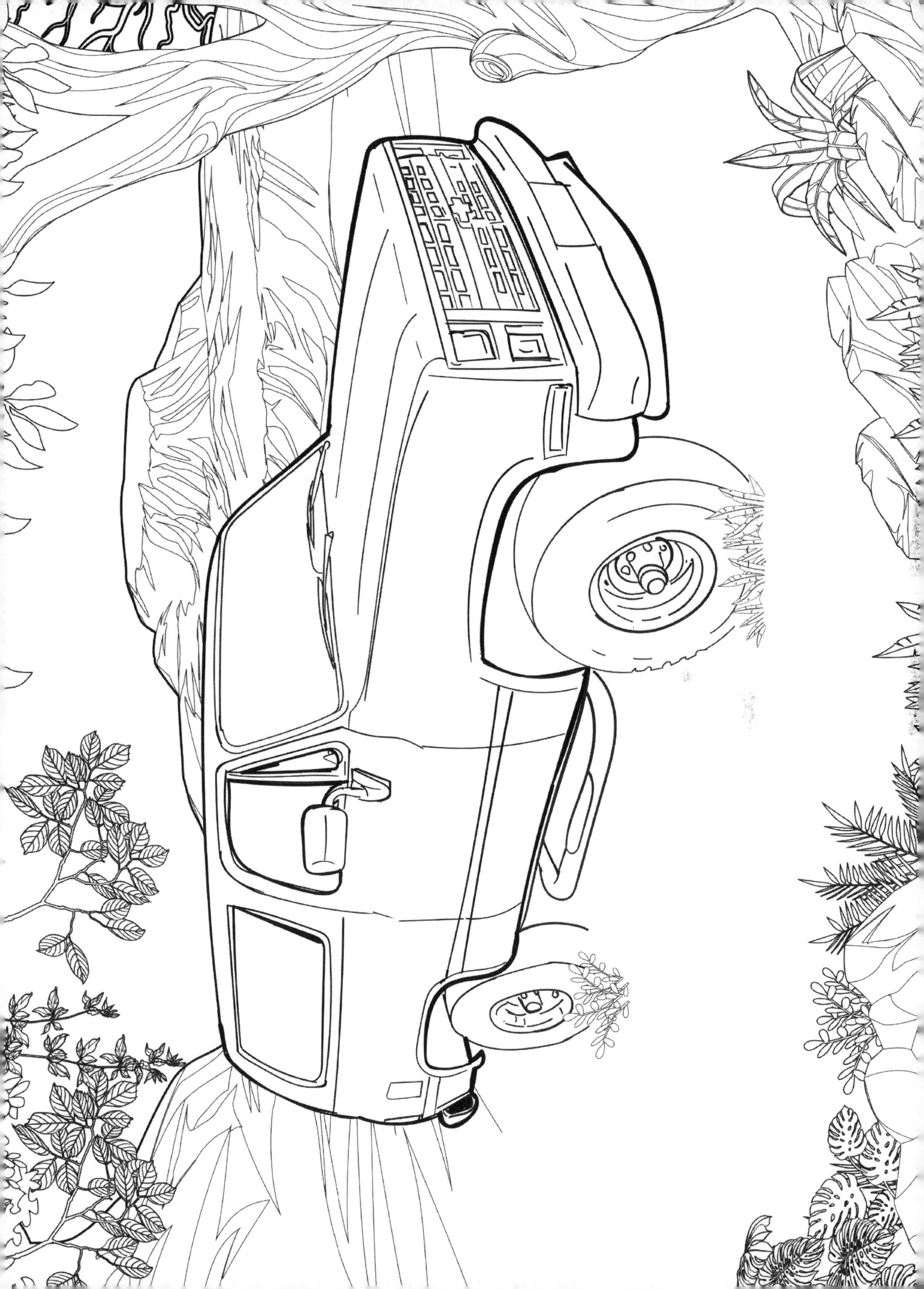

Made in United States
Orlando, FL
16 April 2022

16893929R00057